THIS IS THE TRUE STORY OF
THE 5 SECOND RULE

WHAT it is, **WHY** it works, and **HOW** people around the world are using it to change their lives in five simple seconds.

- The events described in this book are real.
- No names have been changed.
- The social media posts that appear throughout this book are the actual posts.

I cannot wait to share this book with you and watch you unlock the power of you.

5...4...3...2...1...GO!

THE 5 SECOND RULE
TRANSFORM YOUR LIFE, WORK, AND CONFIDENCE WITH EVERYDAY COURAGE

Everyday Courage

Courage is the ability to do things that feel difficult, scary, or uncertain.

It isn't reserved for just a chosen few.

Courage is a birthright. It's inside all of us.

And it's waiting for you to discover it.

One moment of courage can change your day. One day can change your life. And one life can change the world.

That's the true power of courage; it reveals you. The greatest version of you.

Discover your courage, and you will be capable of accomplishing and experiencing anything you dream about.

Yes, even changing the world.

Book 1

PART1

THE 5 SECOND RULE

CHAPTER ONE

FIVE SECONDS TO CHANGE YOUR LIFE

IF YOU'RE SEARCHING FOR

THAT ONE PERSON WHO WILL CHANGE YOUR LIFE

LOOK IN THE MIRROR

You are about to learn something remarkable—it takes just five seconds to change your life. Sounds like a gimmick, doesn't it? It's not. It's science. I'll prove it to you. You change your life one five-second decision at a time. In fact, it's the only way you change.

This is the true story of the 5 Second Rule: what it is, why it works, and how it has transformed the lives of people around the world. The Rule is easy to learn and its impact is profound. It's the secret to changing anything. Once you learn the Rule, you can start using it immediately. The Rule will help you live, love, work, and speak with greater confidence and courage every day. Use it once and it'll be there for you whenever you need it.

I created the 5 Second Rule at a time in my life when everything was falling apart. And by everything, I mean everything: my marriage, finances, career, and self-esteem were all in the gutter. My problems seemed so big that it was a struggle each morning just to get out of bed. That's actually how the Rule began—I invented the Rule to help me break my habit of hitting the snooze button.

When I used the Rule for the very first time seven years ago, I thought it was silly. Little did I know that I had invented a powerful metacognition technique that would change absolutely everything about my life, work, and sense of self.

What's happened to me since discovering the 5 Second Rule and the power of five second decisions is unbelievable. I not only woke up—I shook up my entire life. I've used this one tool to take control and improve everything from my confidence to my cash flow, my marriage to my career, and my productivity to my parenting. I have gone from bouncing checks to seven figures in the bank and from fighting with my husband to celebrating 20 years of marriage. I've cured myself of anxiety, built and sold two small businesses, been recruited to join the teams at CNN and *SUCCESS* magazine, and I'm now one of the most-booked speakers in the world. I've never felt more in control, happy, or free. I couldn't have done any of it without the Rule.

The 5 Second Rule changed everything … by teaching me just one thing: *HOW* to change.

Using the Rule, I replaced my tendency to overthink the smallest moves with a bias toward action. I used the Rule to master self-monitoring and become more present and productive. The Rule taught me how to stop doubting and start believing in myself, my ideas, and my abilities. And, the Rule has given me the inner strength to become a better and much happier person, not for others, but for me.

The Rule can do the same for you. That's why I am so excited to share it with you. In the next few chapters, you'll learn the story behind the Rule, what it is, why it works, and the compelling science to back it up. You'll discover how five second decisions and acts of everyday courage change your life. Finally, you'll learn how you can use the #5SecondRule in combination with the latest research-backed strategies to become healthier, happier, and more productive and effective at work. You'll also learn how to use it to end worry, manage anxiety, find meaning in your life and beat any fear.

And, that's not all. You'll see proof. Lots of proof. This book is packed with social media posts and first-hand accounts from people all over the world who are using the Rule to make some amazing things happen. Yes, the Rule will help you wake up on time, but what it really does is something far more remarkable—**it wakes up the inner genius, leader, rock star, athlete, artist, and change agent inside of you.**

When you first learn the Rule, you'll likely start using it to stick to your goals. You might **use the Rule to push yourself** to get to the gym like Margaret does when she isn't "feeling it."

Or you may **use the Rule to become more influential at work**. That's how Mal first used the Rule—to find the courage to meet with his boss and talk about his career goals (something that so many of us fear). Thanks to the Rule, it not only happened, but it went great:

malzakmeh @mel_robbins, today I made a huge step forward and talked to my boss about my next goal and he totally supported me #5secondrule! Thank you @mel_robbins 😊 😊

That's another thing that's unique about the Rule—I may have created it, but it's not just my story to tell. Inside this book, you'll meet people around the world from all walks of life who are using the Rule, in ways big and small, to take charge of their lives. Their diverse experiences will help you understand just how limitless the applications for the Rule and its benefits truly are.

You can use the Rule to become more productive. Before the 5 Second Rule, Laura used to make endless to-do lists and sat around making excuses and being a jerk to herself. Now, there's no room in Laura's life for excuses—only action. Laura has increased her cash flow by $4,000 a month, finished her bachelor's degree, and hiked a few 4,000 footers. Next up, run a marathon.

 Laura

I heard you speak this past winter and you told me to stop being a jerk to myself, then this happened!!! Thank you for motivating the jerk out of me!

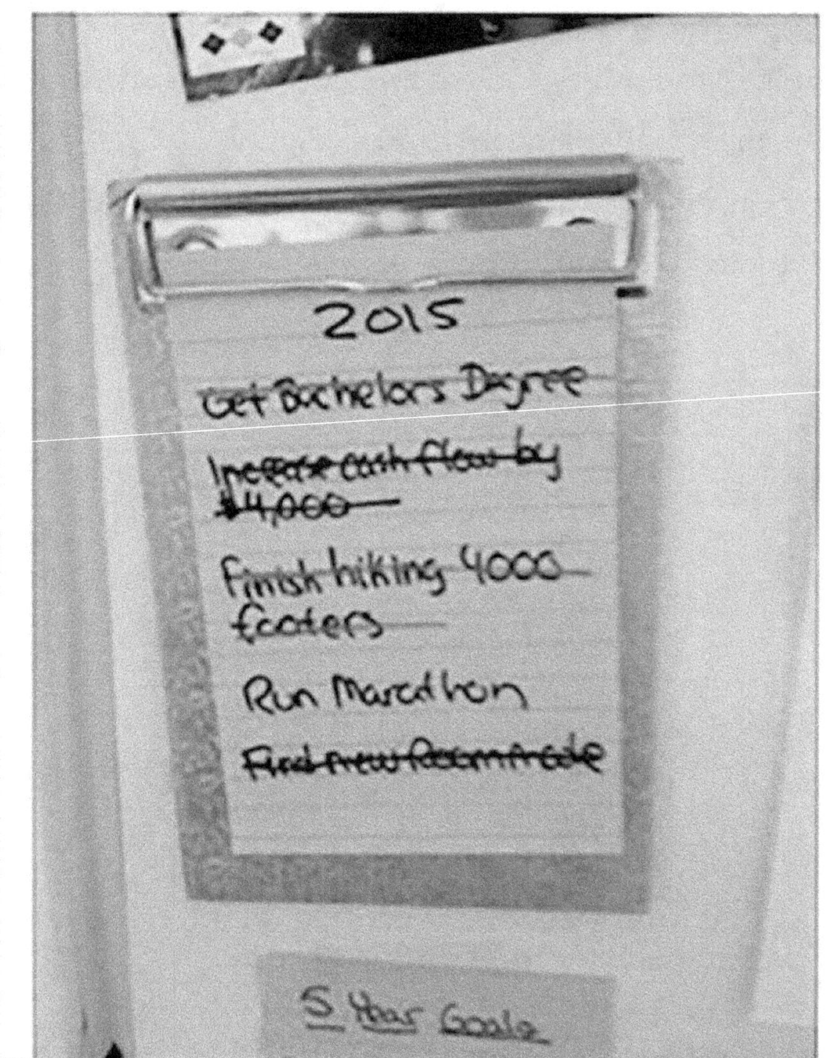

You can use the Rule to step outside of your comfort zone and become more effective at networking. Ken used the 5 Second Rule the same day he learned it at the Project Management Institute National Conference to meet "movers and shakers," Matthew used it to cold-call C-Level executives, and Alan used it to meet "a dozen folks I wouldn't have otherwise" at a PGA Tour event.

Ken Riches @Buckoclown1
@melrobbins Really enjoyed your presentation to PMI NA LIM on Saturday. I have used the 5 second rule at least three times since!

Mel Robbins @melrobbins
@Buckoclown1 how did you use it?!

Ken Riches
@Buckoclown1

@melrobbins twice to introduce myself to movers and shakers, once to get up and get a bunch of work done this AM

Matthew Smith

@melrobbins emailed c-level execs on friends' behalf to get informational interviews. And THEY RESPONDED and everything. 5 sec rule wins!

You can also use the Rule to self-monitor and control your emotions.
Jenna uses the Rule as a mom to practice "patience instead of snapping at" her kids. She's also using it as a sales tool in her new direct selling business. The Rule helps her stop thinking about how "intimidating" it is to sell and gives her the courage to just start selling.

Hi Mel!! Well I really just started putting the 5 second rule into motion. 2 areas of my life I have started really practice using it is with my kids and having the patience instead of snapping at them. I feel like it has given me the extra 5 seconds to put my thoughts together before jumping the gun. Also in building my Yoli business. I take 5 seconds and just ask, just talk to someone and bring up my my business. As u talked about it thinking about the answer rather than thinking about doing it can be very intimidating in this kind of business. Just have to use the 5 seconds and do it instead of thinking about it!! I absolutely loved hearing you in person!!! It was great! Thank you!! I plan to keep putting the 5 second rule in motion throughout many aspects of my life that I want to work on! Hope you have a fabulous day!

Executives inside some of the world's most respected brands are using the Rule to help their managers change, drive sales, engage teams, and innovate. Take Crystal at USAA, whose entire sales team is using the 5 Second Rule and the result has been awesome—they've jumped to "#1 in our location."

Crystal

I have my whole team at USAA doing the 5 second rule so far we have jumped to #1 in our location our goal it to be the number one in the entire company! Here is one of the forms you sent me. I have more to follow.

The #5SecondRule is so easy to learn and so important for confidence that we see managers, like Muz, teaching it to their teams all over the world.

Muz
@muze63

The entire staff glued to a great #TEDtalk by @melrobbins this morning #motivation #5secondrule. Thank you, Mel :)

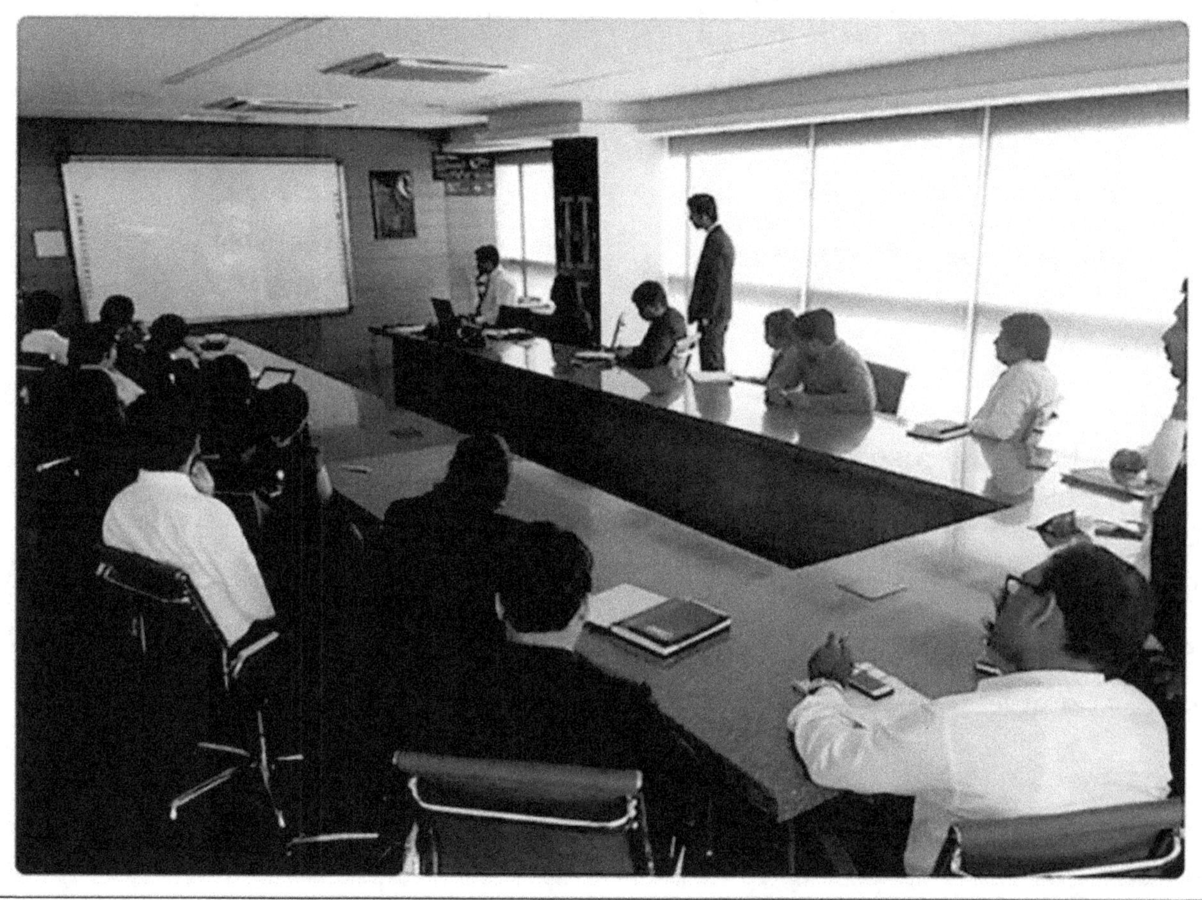

You'll also be inspired by the stories of people who are finding the courage to stop thinking and start putting their ideas into action. Mark, who after decades of thinking about starting a nonprofit ice hockey league for inner city kids, used the Rule to finally get the idea "out of my head" and "into action." He's now partnered with former Olympians and NHL alumni to create camps, clinics, and leagues.

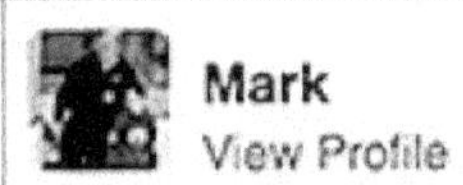

Mark
View Profile

I worked in around the National Hockey League for most of the 1980s and 1990s. I always thought that it was a shame that inner city kids had little access to the sport, which tends to be expensive and impractical for many families.

I always had a concept of hockey legends bringing hockey to the inner city via street hockey. Unfortunately, I put the "emergency break" on each time I had this thought and never followed through with it.

Then in 2013, I watched Mel Robbins TEDx talk and at the 19th minute of a 21-minute presentation, she introduced the "5 second rule."

Bingo!

I immediately got the inner city hockey program out of my head and put it into action. Soon, I joined forces with former US Olympic hockey Star David A. Jensen and the Boston Bruins Alumni to create the "Hockey in the Streets" program, which now conducts camps, clinics and leagues in many urban areas throughout New England.

SAs the program continues to expand, thousands of urban kids will have the chance to experience the great game of hockey. But, it couldn't have happened with the "emergency break" on!
http://www.dajhockey.com/summer-2016-urban-street-hockey-program.html

Summer 2016 Urban Street Hockey Program

The Massachusetts Department of Conservation and Recreation…

dajhockey.com

The Rule is also a powerful tool in the battles of addiction and depression. Bill learned about the #5SecondRule on a Reddit thread and it was the "Right message. Right place. Right time." He started using the Rule's "countdown trick" to quit drinking and it's working "amazing!!" He just celebrated his 40th birthday completely sober.

And it might even save your life A work colleague of mine recently reached out and shared a very poignant #5SecondRule story with me. After he and his wife split up, he fell into a deep depression. It got so bad that he "contemplated suicide." At his lowest point, he used the Rule to "put it down and call for help." Finding the courage to get out of his head by counting 5- 4- 3- 2- 1 and then calling for help saved his life.

Mel, hope all is well. I have been meaning to write you for a while.
As you know I have heard you speak a few times, we have hung out
and I follow your various 'posts'. Know what you do matters. My
wife and I split over a year ago and it has been hard. So hard that I
contemplated suicide, however at my lowest point I said to myself
5-4-3-2-1 put it down and call for help. I am doing great now, life is
good and I have rediscovered my purpose. Never doubt the good
you are doing and the difference you are making. 5-4-3-2-1 go out
and have a great day. Cheers

In using the Rule for more than seven years, and hearing from people all over the world, I've come to realize that every single day we face moments that are difficult, uncertain, and scary. Your life requires courage. And that is exactly what the Rule will help you discover—the courage to become your greatest self.

How Can One Simple Tool Work in So Many Powerful Ways?

Great question. The #5SecondRule is only ever working on one thing—YOU. You have greatness inside of you. Even at your lowest point, greatness is there. The Rule will give you both the clarity to hear that greatness and the courage to act on it.

Using the Rule, I have discovered the courage to do things that I had spent years thinking about and making excuses for. Only through action have I unlocked the power inside of me to become the person that I've always wanted to be. And the confidence I exhibit on TV, online, and on stage is what I call "Real Confidence."

I've built Real Confidence by learning how to honor my instincts with action so that they come to life in the real world. I use the word "honor" on purpose. That's what you are doing when you use the Rule. You are honoring yourself. You are championing your ideas. And each time you use it, you take one step closer to being the person you are truly meant to be. I have changed from the kind of person who just thinks about my ideas to having the confidence to share, act on, and pursue them. If you use the Rule consistently and you honor your instincts with action, the exact same transformation will happen to you.

Marlowe discovered just how easy it is to use the Rule to transform herself. Days after learning the Rule, she used it to stop thinking about signing up for classes and actually do it, which was something she "had been wanting to do but kept making excuses for, for a long time."

Marlowe

Mel!!!! I was a part of the Achievers team when you came and gave a life-changing, earth shattering talk at our ACE conference in Toronto September 14th. I just started reading your book and haven't been able to put it down. In fact, before even getting half way through it, I was reading it in bed one evening and I literally put your book down, got up and drove to York University and signed up for courses- something I had been wanting to do but kept making excuses for, for a long time. It is absolutely incredible and awe-inspiring how easy things become once you wrap your head around your own ability to PUSH yourself. I love you, and I love your book! Your wisdom needs to be shared around the world. You have truly impacted my life in such a short time and I can't even begin to describe how amazing it feels to feel in control. I sincerely hope you come out with another book soon. Sincerely- another grateful fan.

Marlowe

People need to understand just how freaking EASY it is once you actually try it. I'm astonished really. That's why I felt the need to reach out, I know you hear these stories everyday I'm sure but I have literally been procrastinating about signing up for these last 2 courses for years- honestly. And in the middle of your book I was like, what am I waiting for? All I have to do is get in my car and drive 30 minutes to sign up and just do it. So I did. And I'm currently enrolled for this fall semester and winter and I feel challenged and it's exciting! I know that once I accomplish this I'll be looking for my next mountain to climb and I finally feel like I'm doing something for me that will benefit me and what's better is I had the PUSH to do it myself. It feels great. It was a privilege to be able to sit in on your talk, truly! You're an inspiration

As Marlowe put it, "it's absolutely incredible and awe-inspiring how easy things become once you wrap your head around your own ability to PUSH yourself."

She's right. Once you start using the Rule to push yourself out of your head and into action, you'll be "astonished" by how easy it is to make a five second decision that changes everything.

As I used the Rule more and more in my life, I realized that I was making small decisions all day long that held me back. In five seconds flat, I'd decide to stay quiet, to wait, and not to risk it. I'd have an instinct to act and within five seconds my mind would kill it with doubt, excuses, worry, or fear. **I was the problem and in five seconds, I could push myself and become the solution.** The secret to change had been right in front of my face the entire time—five seconds decisions.

Have you ever seen that famous commencement address David Foster Wallace gave at Kenyon College in 2005? If you haven't seen or read this speech, you can find it on YouTube and it's definitely worth the 20 minutes it takes to watch.

In it, Wallace steps up to the mic and starts off with this joke:

There are these two young fish swimming along, and they happen to meet an older fish swimming the other way, who nods at them and says, "Morning, boys, how's the water?"

And the two young fish swim on for a bit, and then eventually one of them looks over at the other and goes, "What the hell is water?"

You can hear the audience laugh in the video, and then Wallace explains the immediate point of the fish story is that *"the most obvious, important realities are often the ones that are the hardest to see and talk about."*

For me, the hardest thing to see and talk about was the very nature of change itself. I had always wondered why it was so damn hard to make myself do the things that I knew I should do in order to expand my career, enrich my relationships, become healthier, and improve my life. Discovering the #5SecondRule gave me the million-dollar answer—change comes down to the courage you need every day to make five second decisions.

You Are One Decision Away from a Completely Different Life

Inside this book, I'm going to share everything that I've learned about change and the power of everyday courage. You're going to love what you are about to learn. The coolest part will be when you start to use the Rule and see the results for yourself. You will not only wake up and realize just how much you've held yourself back. You will also awaken the power that's been inside of you all along.

As you read the stories inside these pages, you might even realize that you've used the #5SecondRule before. If you look back on your life and reflect on some of the most important moments, I guarantee that you've made a life-changing decision purely on instinct. In five seconds flat, you made, what I call, a "heart-first decision." You ignored your fears and let your courage and your confidence speak for you. Five seconds of courage makes all the difference.

Just ask Catherine. When she first learned about the #5SecondRule at her company's executive leadership offsite, it made her realize she had used the Rule to make one of the most important decisions of her life—she just didn't realize it at the time. In 1990, her sister Tracy was killed and Catherine traveled back home to help. That's when "a 5 Second decision" changed not only her life "but so many others as well." She decided to raise her sister's "two little ones" who were "left behind" when Tracy died.

Catherine

Hi Mel,
Can't wait for your book. Makes me appreciate all the great things that have come out of trusting your gut. My sister Tracy was killed by her husband in 1990. Her two little ones were left behind Dan 4 and Trudy 18 months. I came home to help out with the kids........I still remember walking in that day, never having met them and Trudy walked right up to me and gave me a hug. A 5 second decision led to raising them, adopting them, getting married, having a third, and now a grandma to Trudy' 3 kids. 5 seconds not only changes your life but so many others as well. I finally get what a "no brainer" really means. Your heart speaks first and you listen. Thanks for your inspiration. I know I have a story to tell too.
Always a FAN,
Catherine

I love how she describes the decision as a "no brainer"—because when you act with courage, your brain is not involved. Your heart speaks first and you listen. The Rule will teach you how.

Will it take some effort on your part to discover the power within you? Yes, it will. But as Marlowe said just a few pages ago, "It is absolutely incredible and awe-inspiring how easy things become" when you do.

Doing the work to improve your life is simple, you can do it, and it's work you want to do—because it's the most important work that there is. It is the work of learning how to love and trust yourself enough to stop waiting and to start leaning into all the magic, opportunity, and joy that your life, work, and relationships have to offer.

I'm so excited to hear about what happens when you start using the #5SecondRule. But I'm jumping ahead of the story. Before we can talk about all of the exciting ways that you can use the Rule, I need to take you back to 2009 and explain how this all started.

cour-age
/ˈkerij/

noun

- The ability to do something that is difficult or scary
- Stepping outside of your comfort zone
- Sharing your ideas, speaking up, or showing up
- Standing firm in your beliefs and values
- And some days...getting out of bed.

CHAPTER TWO

HOW I DISCOVERED THE 5 SECOND RULE

"COURAGE IS FOUND

IN UNLIKELY PLACES."

J.R.R. TOLKIEN

This all started in 2009. I was 41 years old and facing some major problems with money, work, and in my marriage. As soon as I woke up each morning, all I felt was dread.

Have you ever felt that way? It's the worst. The alarm rings, and you just don't feel like getting up and facing the day. Or, you lie awake at night with your head spinning as you worry about all of your problems.

That was me. For months, I felt so overwhelmed by the problems I had that I could barely get out of bed. When the alarm rang at 6 a.m., I would lie there and think about the day ahead, the lien on the house, the negative account balance, my failed career, how much I resented my husband…and then I would hit the snooze button. Not once, but over and over again.

In the beginning, it wasn't a big deal, but as is the case with any bad habit, as time went on, it snowballed into a much bigger problem that impacted my entire day. By the time I finally got up, the kids had missed the bus and I felt like I was failing at life. I spent most of my days tired, running late, and feeling totally overwhelmed.

I don't even know how it started—I just remember feeling so defeated all the time. My professional life was in the gutter. Over the past 12 years, I had changed careers so many times that I was developing multiple personalities. After graduating from law school, I started my career as a public defender for the Legal Aid Criminal Defense Society in NYC. Then I met my husband Chris and we got married and moved to Boston so that he could pursue his MBA. In Boston, I worked crazy hours for a large law firm and was miserable all the time.

When our daughter was born, I used my maternity leave to look for a new job and landed in the Boston startup scene. I worked for several tech startups during those years. It was fun and I learned a lot but I never felt like tech was the right career for me.

I hired a coach to help me figure out "what to do with my life." Working with a coach led me to want to become one. So, like a lot of people, I worked during the day, focused on the kids when I got home, and then I studied at night to get the certification I needed. Eventually, I launched a coaching business. I loved it, and I would probably still be doing it if the media had not called.

My media career began as a fluke: *Inc.* magazine published an article featuring my coaching business and an executive at CNBC saw it and called. That one call led to lots of meetings. After months of tryouts, I landed a "development deal" with ABC and a call-in radio show on Sirius.

Sounds fancy, but it wasn't. I was surprised to learn that most development deals pay next to nothing and that radio pays even less than that. In reality, I was a mother of three driving back and forth to NYC, sleeping on friends' couches in the city, coaching clients on the side to make the ends meet, leaning too much on friends and family to fill the childcare gaps, and doing whatever I could to make it all work.

After several years scraping by in the media business, I got my "big break." I was cast to host a reality show for FOX. I had visions of magically solving all of our financial problems by becoming a TV star. What a joke. We shot a few episodes of a show called *Someone's Gotta Go*, and then the network tabled the show. In an instant, my media career hit a dead end. I only got paid if we were shooting. I found myself unemployed and locked into a contract for ten months that prevented me from pursuing another media job.

By this point, Chris had finished his MBA and started a thin crust pizza restaurant with his best friend in the Boston area. In the beginning, things were going great. The first location was a home run, the company won Best of Boston™, multiple regional awards, and the pizza was fantastic. They opened up a second restaurant and, on the encouragement of a large grocery chain, a wholesale operation. On the outside, it looked like business was booming. But on the balance sheet, the wheels were starting to come off. They had expanded too quickly. The second restaurant failed and the wholesale business needed more cash to grow. Things got scary very fast.

Like a lot of small business owners, we had poured our home equity line and life savings into the restaurant business and it was now disappearing before our eyes. We had no savings left and the home equity line was fully tapped out. Weeks went by without Chris getting paid. Liens started to hit our house.

With me out of work and Chris's business struggling, the financial pressure mounted; scary letters from attorneys seemed to arrive daily and checks constantly bounced. The collection calls were so relentless that we unplugged the phone. When my dad sent us money to cover the mortgage, I was both grateful and ashamed.

In public, we tried to keep up appearances because so many friends and family members had invested in the restaurant business, which only made the pressure worse. Chris and his partner were working around-the-clock to save it. I tried to keep an upbeat façade, but on the inside I was overwhelmed, embarrassed, and afraid. Our financial problems were tearing us apart. I blamed the restaurants and he blamed me for pursuing a career in the media business. In truth, we were both to blame.

No matter how bad your life can seem, you can always make it worse. I did. I drank too much. Way too much. I was jealous of friends who didn't have to work. I was bitchy and judgmental. Our problems seemed so big that I convinced myself there was nothing I could do. Meanwhile, in public, I just pretended everything was fine.

In hindsight, I can see that is was just easier to feel sorry for myself and blame Chris and his struggling business than to take a look in the mirror and pull myself together. The best way to describe how I felt was "trapped." I felt trapped by my life and the decisions I had made. I felt trapped by our money problems. And I felt trapped in a frustrating struggle with myself.

I knew what I should or could be doing to make things better, but I couldn't make myself do those things. They were small things: getting up on time, being nicer to Chris, getting support from friends, drinking less, and taking better care of myself. But knowing what you need to do isn't enough to create a change.

I would think about exercising, but I wouldn't. I would consider calling a friend to talk, but I didn't. I knew that if I tried to find a job outside of the media industry it would help, but I couldn't motivate myself to look. I didn't feel comfortable going back to coaching people because I felt like such a failure myself.

I knew what I needed to do but I couldn't make myself take action. And that's the thing that makes changing so hard. Change requires you to do things that feel hard and scary. Change requires courage and confidence—and I was tapped out of both.

What I did do was spend a lot of time thinking. Thinking made everything worse. The more I thought about the situation that we were in, the more afraid I felt. That's what your mind does when you focus on problems—it magnifies them. The more I worried, the more uncertain and overwhelmed I became. The more I thought, the more paralyzed I felt.

Every night, I'd have a few drinks to take the edge off. I'd climb in bed drunk or buzzed, close my eyes, and dream about a different life—one where I didn't have to work and all of our problems had magically disappeared. The moment I woke up, I had to face reality: my life was a nightmare. I was 41, unemployed, in financial ruin, struggling with a drinking problem, and had zero confidence in my or my husband's abilities to fix our problems.

That's where the snooze button came in. I hit it…two, three, or four times a morning. When I hit that snooze button it was the one moment every day where I actually felt like I was in control. It was an act of defiance. It was as if I were saying,

*"Oh yeah?! Take that, life! **** you! I'm not getting up right now, I'm going back to sleep. So, there!"*

By the time I finally got up, Chris had already left for the restaurants, the kids were in various states of dress, and the school bus was long gone. To say mornings were chaotic would be putting it politely. They were a train wreck. We were always late. I forgot lunches, backpacks, gym bags, and permission slips as we raced out the door. I felt ashamed by the number of balls I dropped every single day. Feeling that shame just put me on edge even more.

And here's the kicker: I knew what I needed to do to start my day right. I needed to get up on time, make breakfast, and get the kids on the bus. Then I needed to look for a job. It's not like I had to climb Mount Everest. However, the fact that it was simple stuff actually made it worse. I had no legitimate excuse for why I couldn't get it done.

My self-confidence was in a death spiral. If I couldn't even get up on time, how the heck could I have faith in myself to fix the bigger financial and marriage problems that Chris and I faced? Looking back, I can see that I was losing hope.

Have you ever noticed how the smallest things can feel so hard? Having heard from thousands of you, I know that I am not alone on this one. The list of *hard* things is surprisingly universal:

Speaking in a meeting	Hitting "send" on emails	Stepping on a dance floor
Staying positive	Sticking to your plan	Publishing your work
Making a decision	Leaving the house	Getting to the gym
Finding time for yourself	Volunteering to go first	Eating in moderation
Asking for feedback	Showing up at a reunion	Saying "no"
Raising your hand	Blocking an ex on social media	Asking for help
Asking for a raise	Talking to someone you find attractive	Letting your guard down
Ending self-doubt		Admitting you are wrong
Working on your résumé		Listening

In my case, it was getting up on time. Lying in bed every night, I would make promises to myself that tomorrow I would change:

Tomorrow, I will change. Tomorrow, I will wake up earlier. Tomorrow, I will have a better attitude and try a little harder. I will go to the gym. I'll be nice to my husband. I'll eat healthy. I won't drink so much. Tomorrow I will be the future me!

And with that vision in mind and a heart full of hope, I'd set my alarm for 6 a.m. and close my eyes. And the cycle would begin the very next morning. As soon as that alarm rang, I didn't feel like the "future me." I felt like the old me, and the old me wanted to keep sleeping.

Yes, I thought about getting up, and then I would hesitate, roll toward the alarm, and hit the snooze button. Five seconds was all it took for me to talk myself out of it.

The reason that I didn't get out of bed was simple: I just didn't *feel like it*. I would later learn that I was stuck in what researchers call a "habit loop." I had hit the snooze button so many mornings in a row the behavior was now a closed-loop pattern encoded in my brain.

Then one night, everything changed.

I was about to turn off the TV and head to bed when a television commercial caught my attention. There on the screen was the image of a rocket launching. I could hear the famous final five-second countdown, 5- 4- 3- 2- 1, fire and smoke filled the screen, and the shuttle launched.

I thought to myself, *"That's it, I'll launch myself out of bed tomorrow…like a rocket. I'll move so fast I won't have time to talk myself out of it."* It was just an instinct. One that I could have easily dismissed. Luckily, I didn't. I acted on it.

The fact is, I wanted to solve our problems. I didn't want to destroy my marriage or keep feeling like the world's worst mom. I wanted to be financially secure. I wanted to feel happy and proud of myself again.

And I Desperately Wanted to Change. I Just Didn't Know How.

And this is an important point in my story. This instinct to launch myself out of bed was my inner wisdom talking. Hearing it was a tipping point. Following its instructions was life-changing. Your brain and your body send you signals to wake up and to pay attention. This idea of launching myself out of bed is an example of that. Your instincts may seem stupid in the moment, but when you honor them with deliberate action, it can change your life.

There's more to this point about acting on your instincts than just the phrase "trust your gut." New research from the University of Arizona, in partnership with Cornell and Duke, has shown that there's a powerful connection between your brain and your instinct to act. When you set a goal, your brain opens up a task list. Whenever you are near things that can help you achieve those goals, your brain fires up your instincts to signal to get that goal completed. Let me give you an example.

Let's say you have a goal to get healthier. If you walk into a living room, nothing happens. If you walk past a gym, however, your prefrontal cortex lights up because you are near something related to getting healthier. As you pass the gym, you'll feel like you *should* exercise. That's an instinct reminding you of the goal. That's your inner wisdom, and it's important to pay attention to it, no matter how small or silly that instinct may seem.

Subconsciously, my brain was signaling me to pay attention to this rocket launch on TV. In that five-second moment, my brain was sending me a very clear set of instructions:

Pay attention to that rocket launch, Mel. Grab the idea. Believe in it. And do it. Don't stop and think. Don't talk yourself out of it. Launch yourself out of bed tomorrow, Mel.

That's one of the things I've learned using the #5SecondRule. When it comes to goals, dreams, and changing your life, your inner wisdom is a genius. Your goal-related impulses, urges, and instincts are there to guide you. You need to learn to bet on them. Because, as history proves, you'll never know when your greatest inspiration will strike and where that discovery will lead you if you trust yourself enough to act on it.

This is how some of the world's most useful inventions were discovered. In 1826, John Walker discovered the match while he was using a stick to stir a pot of chemicals, and when he tried to scrape a gob off the end—it ignited. He followed his instinct to try to recreate it and this is how he discovered the match. In 1941, George de Mestral invented Velcro® after noticing how easily cockleburs attached to his dog's fur. In 1974, Art Fry got the idea for the Post-It® Note because he needed a bookmark that would stay put on a page in his hymnal until Sunday's church service, but that would not damage the pages when he removed it.

That's even how the Frappuccino was born. In 1992, an assistant manager at a Starbucks in Santa Monica noticed that sales dropped whenever it was hot outside. He had an instinct to make a frozen drink and he followed it, asking for a blender, tinkering with recipes, and giving a Vice President a sample. The first Frappucino rolled out in his store a year later.

When it comes to change, goals, and dreams, you have to bet on yourself. That bet starts with hearing the instinct to change and honoring that instinct with action. I feel so thankful that I listened to my dumb idea about launching myself out of bed like a rocket because everything in my life changed as a result of it. Here's what happened:

The next morning the alarm rang at 6 a.m. and the first thing I felt was dread. It was dark. It was cold. It was winter in Boston and I did not want to wake up. I thought about the rocket launch and I immediately felt like it was stupid. Then, I did something that I had never done before—**I ignored how I felt. I didn't think. I did what needed to be done**

Instead of hitting the snooze button, I started counting.

Backwards.

5..4..3..2..1..

And then I stood up.

That was the exact moment I discovered the #5SecondRule.

The 5 Second Rule

The moment you have an **instinct** to **act on a goal**
you must

5-4-3-2-1

and **physically move** or your **brain will stop** you.

CHAPTER THREE

WHAT YOU CAN EXPECT WHEN YOU USE IT

"IT MATTERS NOT WHAT SOMEONE

IS BORN, BUT WHAT THEY GROW TO BE."

J.K. ROWLING

When I used the Rule that first morning, I was as surprised as you are that something that stupid worked. Counting backwards? 5- 4- 3- 2- 1… seriously? I didn't know why it worked. I just knew it did. I had struggled for months to wake up on time and suddenly the #5SecondRule made changing my behavior simple.

Later I would learn that when you count backwards, you mentally shift the gears in your mind. You interrupt your default thinking and do what psychologists call "assert control." The counting distracts you from your excuses and focuses your mind on moving in a new direction. When you physically move instead of stopping to think, your physiology changes and your mind falls in line. In researching this book, I discovered that the Rule is (in the language of habit research) a "starting ritual" that activates the prefrontal cortex, helping to change your behavior.

The prefrontal cortex is the part of your brain that you use when you focus, change, or take deliberate actions. I knew what the prefrontal cortex was, but I would soon learn through my research about the basal ganglia, habit loops, activation energy, behavior flexibility, cognitive biases, neural plasticity, the progress principle, and locus of control. I certainly didn't realize I had just discovered a singular technique that impacted all of them.

I used the Rule the next morning, and it worked again. And then a funny thing happened: I started to see five-second moments all day long, just like my struggle to wake up on time. If I stopped to think about what I knew I needed to do, I was toast. It took less than five seconds for excuses to flood my mind and for my own brain to stop me.

As you use the Rule, you'll see it too—there is a five-second window between your initial instinct to act and your brain stopping you. Seeing the five-second window changed everything for me. The problem was very clear. It was me. I was holding myself back, five seconds at a time.

So I made myself a simple promise: If I knew that I should do something that could change me for the better, then I would use the Rule to push myself to do it, *regardless of how I felt*. I started using the Rule to force myself to not only get up early, but also to get to the gym, look for a job, drink less, and be a better parent and wife.

> If I started to feel too tired to exercise, I would
>
> > 5- 4- 3- 2- 1 and push myself out the door for a run.
>
> If I started pouring a drink that I shouldn't have, I'd
>
> > 5- 4- 3- 2- 1 and put down the bottle of bourbon and walk away.

If I felt myself being bitchy with Chris, I'd

> 5- 4- 3- 2- 1 and correct my tone and make myself be kinder.

If I caught myself procrastinating, I'd

> 5- 4- 3- 2- 1 and sit down and start working on my résumé.

What I discovered is powerful: pushing yourself to take simple actions creates a chain reaction in your confidence and your productivity. By pushing yourself to take the simple steps of moving your life forward, you create momentum and experience a sense of freedom and power that's hard to accurately describe. Rachel found that the "simple step" of getting up on time "started a chain of events" that led to her losing "30 pounds, bought my first home, and reinvigorated my marriage."

From: Rachel

Message Body:
You've helped me change my life and we've never even met. Since watching your Ted Talk a few months ago I've lost 30 pounds, bought my first home, and reinvigorated my marriage. I have no idea if you'll actually see this (I imagine you get a lot of mail), but I needed to thank you for the simple challenge of getting up 30 minutes earlier. That simple step started a chain of events that have made all the difference for me.

Rachel used the word "reinvigorated," and that's exactly what the Rule does. Rebecca had the same experience. By using the Rule to 5- 4- 3- 2- 1 and push herself to make small moves forward, she's breaking out of a mental jail. No longer trapped by analysis paralysis, Rebecca feels "FREE for the 1st time in 47 years!"

Rebecca

I finally feel FREE for the 1st time in 47yrs!!!!

For the 1st time I BELIEVE IN ME....for the 1st time I LOVE ME!

There's an important concept in psychology put forth by Julian Rotter in 1954. It's called "locus of control." The more that you believe that you are in control of your life, your actions and your future, the happier and more successful you'll be. There's one thing that is guaranteed to increase your feelings of control over your life: a bias toward action.

Forget motivation; it's a myth. I don't know when we all bought into the idea that in order to change you must "feel" eager or "feel" motivated to act. It's complete garbage. The moment it's time to assert yourself, you will not feel motivated. In fact, you won't feel like doing anything at all. If you want to improve your life, you'll need to get off your rear end and kick your own butt. In my world, I call that the power of a push.

One of the reasons why the #5SecondRule is so empowering is because it turns you into the kind of person who operates with a bias toward action. If you tend to overthink every move, you'll discover the energy and confidence to stop thinking and actually move. Using the Rule strengthens your belief that you *do* have the ability to control your own fate—because you are proving it to yourself one push at a time.

Jenney is finally taking control of her health. She realized that when she would eat a meal of "canned raviolis, a bag of chips, and a soda…then complain about being overweight," she was sabotaging her efforts to lose weight. By committing to "5- 4- 3- 2- 1-HEALTHY," Jenney was able to use the Rule to give herself the "kick in the arse" she needed.

I already started this morning! My alarm clock went off this morning and I hit snooze, THEN said, "5-4-3-2-1 GO!" and got out of bed.
I had to stop at the store for lunch on my way to work. I normally get canned raviolis, a bag of chips, and a soda...then complain about being overweight. Right before I walked in the store, I said, "5-4-3-2-1 HEALTHY" and got a sandwich and a water.

I need to lose 90 to 100 pounds and starting TODAY I am going to do it! I am not going to wait till...the first day of the month, the last day of the month, Monday, Friday, or whatever future date I tell myself will work. I am starting TODAY and I want to thank YOU for being my motivation/kick in the arse I needed!

When Donna first learned the Rule at an Aveda Institute Conference she thought, "Yeah, yeah I'll use it, but it's not going to be life changing…" That's how I felt about the Rule too—that I'd just use it as a trick to beat the snooze alarm. Boy, was I wrong! So was Donna; it changed just about everything in her life and business. As Donna found, "Only we can hold ourselves back. It's amazing to see how horribly I held myself hostage out of fear and where I am today. More importantly, where I see myself in years to come."

Donna

While still a student at the Aveda Institute Tallahassee I sacrificed many things in order to afford a ticket and travel to "Serious Business" in New Orleans. Those choices and determination changed my life in a dramatic way.

At "Serious Business" I heard incredible speakers that inspired me right at the transition point of my career. Mel spoke about the 5 Second Rule and at the time I thought yeah yeah I'll use it but it's not going to be life changing. I slowly started using it in small daily tasks: "I want to stay in bed… ugh ok 5-4-3-2-1" and I would get up and start my day. Then it subconsciously became a habit. It built confidence within me I didn't know I had.

*My boss/mentor asked me to be a salon mentor. I was one of the newest in the salons yet I was given to opportunity to coach on new products to our team members. 5-4-3-2-1-Go! Coach with confidence.

*I want to be an Aveda educator and instead of waiting on the opportunity to take classes I made that opportunity a reality. I asked my boss/mentor for a meeting to discuss to possibility and now I'm on the track for taking classes and making my dream a reality. 5-4-3-2-1-Go! Don't be afraid to ask the universe for what you want in life.

*At "Dare to Dream" an Aveda conference while sitting in the audience I thought I was covering my eyes from the stage lights when the speakers on stage thought I volunteered to speak in front of the entire venue. When they brought me the microphone I panicked for a moment. 5-4-3-2-1-Go! Be brave. Don't say no to opportunities even if you blindly stumbled upon them.

5-4-3-2-1-Go! Whatever I'm faced with - just go. My career has become so much more with making myself step off the ledge boldly. Even though in the beginning I felt like I tripped over the edge or praying someone would help pull me over. I've realized the more times I step boldly and didn't say no to opportunities the more my confidence is built and the easier it is to say yes to my future. Only we can hold ourselves back. It's amazing to see how horribly I held myself hostage out of fear and where I am today. More importantly where I see myself in the years to come. Go! Do! Say yes in… 5-4-3-2-1.

"If you're going to doubt something, doubt your limits." -Mel Robbins.

As you use the Rule more and more, you'll begin to feel courage, confidence, pride, and a sense of control. The Rule has that effect. I often tell people "the Rule will haunt you," and I mean it—just ask Darryl.

That's because you'll realize you've been sleepwalking through life for a long time. Something this simple, easy, and effective is also contagious. Crystal has already started using it with her son:

The first person I told about the Rule was my husband. Chris had definitely noticed the changes, in particular that my bitchy demeanor was melting and that I was actually being proactive. It didn't take much to convince him that there was a "secret weapon" mentality he was living without.

He adopted the Rule and used it to make some major changes. He quit drinking, started meditating daily, and exercising every morning. The Rule doesn't make these things easy; it makes them happen. That's why I describe it as a tool.

Instead of avoiding the creditor calls and bankruptcy letters, we 5- 4- 3- 2- 1 to hit it head on. I used 5- 4- 3- 2- 1 to push myself to reach out to old coaching clients to rev up the referral engine. I used 5- 4- 3- 2- 1 to propel myself to go on interviews for radio hosting gigs, despite the contract issues with FOX. Together we 5- 4- 3- 2- 1 to push ourselves to meet with accountants and financial advisors to restructured our debt and do the nauseating work to face the hole we had dug, and get disciplined about slowly crawling our way out of it.

Chris brought the Rule into his business to push himself through fear, guilt, and uncertainty. He and his partner met with dozens of advisors, crunched financial models, worked day and night until they closed the wholesale business, and grew their retail locations enabling them to sell off select locations and pay back as many investors and creditors that they could. It's remarkable what Chris and Jonathan did. Grit, hustle, and commitment. They pushed, pushed, and pushed some more.

To this day, when Chris reflects on the restaurant days, his mind will sometimes drift toward feeling like a failure. When he catches himself thinking those negative thoughts, he uses 5- 4- 3- 2- 1 to redirect his mind to think about what they did build: seven restaurants, an incredible employee culture, millions in revenue, and a remarkable brand. Did it end up how he had dreamt? No, it didn't. But what he learned about business, partnership, and himself during the process is worth more than money can buy.

There's nothing more powerful than the feeling of confidence and pride you gain when you keep trudging forward, face life's challenges head on, and push yourself to change for the better. As Chris put it, "the Rule helped me process the experience of succeeding and failing—on so many levels. Ultimately, this awareness gave me power and control over my positive and negative thoughts."

As we started to reconnect with friends, the Rule would often come up. You'll find that too. Jennifer learned the Rule and told her nurse about it. Her nurse's response? "You have no idea how many times I'll need to do this a day."

I was talking to my nurse about my amazing trip to Nashville and was telling her about Mel Robbins 5-4-3-2-1 rule and she was blown away and going to start doing it. She said "you have no idea how many times I'll need to do this in a day." #54321 #justdoit #besomeonescheerleader #inspire #conqueryourfears

The Rule ignites something powerful in everyone who tries it. One of our friends had the courage to ask for a divorce and another left his consulting job for one that didn't require travel. A work pal lost 73 pounds and my uncle stopped talking about giving up smoking and finally quit. A friend of Chris's moved back to Maine and used the Rule to negotiate an awesome job working remotely.

The #5SecondRule gave them all what it had given me: the framework, the courage, and the method for HOW to push yourself to change.

The first time I shared the Rule in public was in 2011 during a TEDx Talk entitled "*How to Stop Screwing Yourself Over.*" The funny thing is that the talk was mostly about my dream (back then) of becoming a top talk radio show host and how I help people live the lives that they really want. I only mention the #5SecondRule at the very end of the speech, and I barely even explain it. What happened next was crazy. The talk went viral. Millions of people watched it online. And that's not all. They started writing.

Every single day, I hear from people around the world who are using the Rule, just like Mark. Mark is using it to create some pretty incredible changes in just 6 months:

fujfocus Just so you know, with the help of 5SR and your inspiration, I'm doing so much in the last six months, like on pace to double my business in two years, writing a book on business sale and then another one on 100 days outside of my comfort zone, finding and being with the woman beyond my dreams @amyazzarito, being closer with my kids than ever. and making plans to explore the world.

It's the coolest thing. More than 100,000 people in more than 80 countries, to date, have written to me about their experiences using it. As more and more people started to write with questions and requests for more information, I began to research the Rule in depth so that I could better explain the many ways you can use it and prove why it works. I'm a lawyer by profession, so I really went nuts on the research. I looked for precedent, evidence, and guidance as if I were going to have to prove my case about the #5SecondRule to a jury.

It took me almost three years. I read everything I could find on the subject of change, happiness, habits, motivation, and human behavior. I read social science experiments, happiness research, books on the brain, and neuroscience studies. I didn't limit my research to the "experts;" I sent questionnaires to everyday people, like you and me, who were using the Rule. Then I got on the phone, Skype, and

Google Chat, and dug into the step-by-step experiences of what someone faces the moment they choose to change.

As I deconstructed the moment of change, I uncovered something fundamental about how each and every one of us is wired. Right before we're about to do something that feels difficult, scary or uncertain, we hesitate. Hesitation is the kiss of death. You might hesitate for a just nanosecond, but that's all it takes. That one small hesitation triggers a mental system that's designed to stop you. And it happens in less than—you guessed it—five seconds.

Ever notice how fast fear and self-doubt take over your head and you start making up excuses for why you shouldn't say something or do something? We hold ourselves back in the smallest, most mundane moments every day, and that impacts everything. If you break this habit of hesitating and you find the courage to "take some kind of action," you'll be astonished by how fast your life changes. That's what Keith discovered after learning the Rule at a RE/MAX convention. Now he's able to "do extraordinary things."

Keith Pike Mel, I first heard of you in 2015. Then I had the pleasure of seeing you live at the RE/MAX convention in Las Vegas in February 2016. You've inspired me to be able to do extraordinary things. I just had to get out of my own way and take action. In 18 months, I have achieved unbelievable success by opening 3 offices and recruiting more than 50 agents in lil ole Arkansas. No more hesitation, no more procrastination. I take some kind of action and it helps launch me to my goal. A large task suddenly becomes manageable. The hardest part is starting. Thank you, for sharing your story and for encouraging us to be the best versions of ourselves.

You see, it's not the big moves that define our lives; it's the smallest ones. Within five seconds of stopping to think, you'll have decided not to take any action on those small things. Over time, those small decisions build. And here's the kicker: We've repeated this pattern of hesitating, worrying, and doubting ourselves so much, that these actions are now habits that have encoded in our brains.

The fact that hesitating, holding yourself back, and overthinking are habits is good news. There's a simple, proven way to break or replace bad habits and the #5SecondRule is the easiest way to do it. Once you read about habit loops, starting rituals, activation energy, and the role that feelings play in triggering your decisions, you'll appreciate the magnitude of the #5SecondRule. As you use the Rule, you'll see how change hinges on five second decisions and just how easily you can take back control.

The Rule will work every time you use it. But you have to use it. It is a tool. If you stop using it, fear and uncertainty will creep back in and take control of your decisions. If that happens, just start using the Rule again.

As you use the Rule over time, you'll experience a shift inside yourself that is much deeper, a transformation that impacts confidence and inner strength. You will come face to face with the excuses, habits, feelings, insecurities, and fears that have haunted you for years. You will see the bullshit you put yourself through every day and how much precious time you waste waiting for things to change.

By using the Rule, that waiting will end. You will be absolutely amazed by how much joy and freedom you feel by making five-second decisions. Freedom is exactly how Robin described what she gets from using the Rule.

@melrobbins thx 4 the life-changing
#5SecondRule there is freedom in taking action.

Robin

@melrobbins my passion & vision 4 making a difference R huge my confidence sometimes lags. When in doubt I apply #5SecondRule #BizPridePiper

And that's what I've gained too—life-changing freedom. The person I was seven years ago ... is gone. And that's a good thing. Every phase of your life and career will require a different you. Using the Rule, you'll become the person you're meant to become in this next phase of your life.

So, what do you say we dig into the basics of the Rule so you can start using it?

 **Mel Robbins** ✓
@melrobbins

Knowing what you need to do to improve your life takes wisdom. Pushing yourself to do it takes courage. #5SecondRule

CHAPTER FOUR

WHY THE RULE WORKS

"YOU CAN CHOOSE COURAGE OR YOU CAN CHOOSE COMFORT, BUT YOU CANNOT HAVE BOTH."

BRENÉ BROWN

Over the years, I've received lots of questions about the #5SecondRule. I wanted to start your introduction to using the Rule by answering some of the most frequently asked question I've received about this awesome tool.

What Exactly Is the #5SecondRule?

The Rule is a simple, research-backed metacognition tool that creates immediate and lasting behavior change. Metacognition, by the way, is just a fancy word for any technique that allows you to beat your brain in order to accomplish your greater goals.

How Do I Use the Rule?

Using the Rule is simple. Whenever you feel an instinct fire up to act on a goal or a commitment, or the moment you feel that yourself hesitate on doing something and you know you *should* do, use the Rule.

Start by counting backwards to yourself: 5- 4- 3- 2- 1. The counting will help you focus on the goal or commitment and distract you from the worries, thoughts, and fears in your mind. As soon as you reach "1," move. That's it. It's so simple but let me hammer this home one more time. Anytime there's something *you know you should do*, but you feel uncertain, afraid, or overwhelmed…just take control by counting backwards 5- 4- 3- 2- 1. That'll quiet your mind. Then, move when you get to "1."

Counting and moving are actions. By teaching yourself to take action when normally you'd stop yourself by thinking, you can create remarkable change. Counting backwards does a few important things simultaneously: It distracts you from your worries, it focuses your attention on what you need to do, it prompts you to act, and it interrupts the habits of hesitating, overthinking, and holding yourself back.

If you are wondering if the Rule works if you count forward 1- 2- 3- 4- 5, instead of backwards 5- 4- 3- 2- 1, the answer is no—it doesn't. Just ask Trent.

Trent Kruessel

Mel,

Pertaining to the 5 second rule, I've also found that it doesn't work if I count from 1 to 5. If I do that, I am tempted to say "6" and then the action is stalled. I have to count down from 5 to 1 because the next word in my mind (after 1) is "BLASTOFF". And that is definitely an action word.

Just my take.

As Trent discovered, if you count up, you can keep counting. When you count backwards 5- 4- 3- 2…there is nowhere to go after you reach "1," so it is a prompt to move.

Why Is It Called the #5SecondRule?

I get this question a lot. And I wish I had a better answer. I called it the "#5SecondRule" because that's the first thing that popped into my mind the morning I first used it, and this nam stuck. Remember, I had seen a rocket launch the night before and thought to myself, "I'll just launch myself out of bed—like a rocket!" The next morning, I counted backwards 5- 4- 3- 2- 1—because that's what NASA does when it launches a spaceship. I started with 5 for no particular reason other than it felt like the right amount of time to give myself.

I've come to learn that there are a lot of other "5 second rules" in the world, like the one about eating food off the floor, the five-second shot clock in basketball, the game Ellen DeGeneres plays on her talk show, and the five-second test you can do to see if a sidewalk's surface is too hot for your dog to walk on.

Had I known my Rule would spread around the world, I might have come up with a more original name. But in hindsight, all these #5SecondRules have something in common. They require you to physically move within a five-second window.

Physical movement is the most important part of my Rule, too, because when you move your physiology changes and your mind follows. Perhaps the name is not only apropos—it's actually perfect because it references other five-second windows in life, and that makes the Rule feel that much more familiar, universal, and true.

The Rule Sounds Like Nike's Tagline "Just Do It"...

The difference between "Just Do It" and the #5SecondRule is simple. "Just Do It" is a concept—it's *what* you need to do. The #5SecondRule is a tool—it's *how* you make yourself do it.

There's a reason why "Just Do It" is the most famous tagline in the world and resonates across all cultures. Do you know what makes the tagline so powerful? It's the word "JUST."

The word JUST is in there because Nike recognizes something we've talked a lot about in this book—right before we act, we first stop and think. "Just Do It" acknowledges that we're all struggling to push ourselves to be better and do better. We all hesitate and wrestle with our feelings before we jump in. The word JUST tells us that we're not alone. Every single one of us has these small hesitations.

It's the moment right before you ask to join the pick-up game that's already underway, the moment you contemplate whether to do a third set of reps, or when you start to question whether you'll head out the door for a run in the pouring rain.

The tagline acknowledges that you have excuses and fears and Nike is encouraging you to be bigger than them. *Come on…don't think about it…JUST DO IT. I know you're tired…JUST DO IT. I know you are afraid…JUST DO IT.*

Nike's tagline is pushing you to move past that doubt and get in the game. Nike knows that there's greatness inside of you, and it's on the other side of your excuses. It resonates profoundly because every single one of us, even an Olympic athlete, needs a PUSH. And that's where the #5SecondRule comes in; the Rule is *how* you push yourself when no coach, competitor, parent, screaming fan, or teammate is there to push you. With the Rule, you just 5- 4- 3- 2- 1 to push yourself.

Is There a Five-Second Window of Opportunity for Everyone?

Yes. There is a window for everyone between the moment you have an instinct to change and your mind killing that instinct. While your mind starts working against you in nanoseconds, the barrage of thoughts and excuses don't seem to kick into full force and stop you for a few seconds. The five-second window seems to work for everyone.

That said, by all means play around with it to make it work for you. Personally, I notice that the longer I wait between my initial impulse to act and physically moving, the louder that the excuses get, and the harder it becomes to force myself to move. As Angela found, those five-second decisions "turned into 50 seconds and then 500 seconds when the fear was deeper." She now treats the #5SecondRule as if her brain will "self-destruct" at zero:

> Angela Rae Hughes I was there and I have to thank you for that speech. I am back at home now in Seattle and want you to know that YOU moved me to take action on something I have been procrastinating because of deep self doubt and fear of failure. I had the realization that I have always used the 5-second rule in my life without recognizing it... But I also realized that those 5 seconds turned into 50 seconds and then 500 seconds when the fear was deeper. You taught me that my brain will shut it down after 5-seconds so now I have decided to treat the 5-second rule as if it will 'self destruct' (for lack of a better explanation) at zero so I better MAKE THAT MOVE! Thank you kindly, Mel Robbins, for your wisdom.

If it works for you to shorten or lengthen the window, personalize the Rule to make it work for you.

Matt, a good friend of my husband and myself, was training for his first Tough Mudder race. He lives in New Jersey and he sent this text to my husband during the freezing cold winter. He had shrunk the window to three seconds because he noticed how fast his mind would go to work to stop him.

"Tell your girlfriend Mel that the 5 second rule is working over here. I have it down to three seconds. Why contemplate life's complexities when you can be moving ahead after just 3 seconds. In 5 seconds I can make up at least 2 excuses in my mind. In three seconds my mind has already pushed the first button on my phone to move the ball ahead. As I awoke this morning I mistakenly checked the thermometer (that took 2 seconds, but in that third second I started to put on my right sneaker."

That is how the system in your brain works—the longer that you think about something, the lower your urge to act becomes. We are amazing at fooling ourselves into staying exactly where we are. As soon as that impulse to act kicks in, you start rationalizing it away. That's why you've got to move faster—so you can break free of your excuses before your mind traps you.

What Can I Use It For?

Over the years, we've heard thousands of examples of how people are using the Rule to improve their life, relationships, happiness, and work. But every example falls into one of three distinct categories for how you can use it.

• You Can Use It to Change Your Behavior

You can use the Rule to push yourself to create new habits, pull yourself away from destructive habits, and master the skills of self-monitoring and self-control so that you can be more intentional and effective in your relationships with yourself and others.

• You Can Use It to Act with Everyday Courage

You can use the Rule to discover the courage you need to do things that are new, scary, or uncertain. The Rule will quiet your self-doubt and build confidence as you push yourself to pursue your passions, share your ideas at work, volunteer for projects that stretch you, create your art, and become a better leader.

• You Can Use It to Control Your Mind

You can use the Rule to stop the barrage of negative thoughts and endless worries that weigh you down. You can also break the habit of anxiety and beat any fear. When you take control of your mind, you'll be able to think about things that bring you joy instead of focusing on the negative. And that, in my opinion, is the most powerful way to use the Rule.

Why Does Something So Simple Work?

The Rule works because it is so simple. There are all kinds of tricky ways your brain kills your urge to act. Some of my most favorite researchers, professors, and thinkers have written bestsellers and delivered epic TED Talks detailing how our own minds betray us with a seemingly endless list of tricks including cognitive biases, the paradox of choice, the psychological immune system, and the spotlight effect. What all these great researchers have taught me is that the moment you want to change, break a habit, or do something hard or scary, your brain goes to work to stop you.

Basically, your mind tricks you into thinking things through. And the moment you get tricked into doing this, you'll get trapped by your thoughts. Your mind has a million ways to talk you out of acting. That's the neurological reason why it's so hard to change. As I mentioned in Chapter One, change requires you to do things that are uncertain, scary, or new. Your brain, by design, will not let you do such things. Your brain is afraid of things that feel uncertain, scary, or new, so it will do whatever it can to talk you out of doing those things. It is part of your hard-wiring, and this hesitation happens really fast. That is why you have to act even faster to beat it.

The Rule leverages and is an example of some powerful and proven principles in modern psychology: a bias toward action, internal locus of control, behavioral flexibility, the progress principle, starting rituals, the Golden Rule of Habits, authentic pride, deliberate action, "If-Then planning," and activation energy. Throughout this book, you'll learn more about these principles as we go into greater detail about how you can use the Rule in specific areas of your life.

How Can One Rule Work On So Many Areas of My Life?

The #5SecondRule actually only works on one thing—*you*. You stop yourself from changing the exact same way every single time—you hesitate, then you overthink, and you lock yourself in mental jail.

That moment of hesitation is a killer. Hesitation sends a stress signal to your brain. It's a red flag that signals something's wrong—and your brain is goes into protection mode. This is how we are wired to fail. Think about this for a minute.

You don't hesitate all time. For example, you don't hesitate when you pour a cup of coffee in the morning. You don't hesitate when you put on your jeans. You don't hesitate when you turn on the television. You don't hesitate to call your best friend. You don't think at all. You just have the instinct to call your friend, and you pick up the phone, and you call them. But when you hesitate just before making a sales call or texting someone back, it makes your brain think that something must be wrong. The longer you think about that sales call, the less likely you'll make it.

Most of us don't even realize how often we hesitate because we've done it so often that it's become a habit. Here's how Tim described it after using the Rule:

"Honestly, I think the Rule is powerful simply because keeping it on the tip of your thoughts allows you to process and start on activities you would normally gloss over and ignore. I also keep saying, "What the hell, I'm leaning into this." So, it is powerful because it helps you break the formally embedded thought patterns about doing things and allows (me anyway) to safely 'go for it'. Seriously, why was I afraid of doing some of the things I am now doing? It was never like anything I did or didn't do was going to end the world."

But what you will soon learn is that moment of hesitation can also be used to your advantage. Every time you catch yourself hesitating, it is a push moment! The five-second window is opened and it is time to 5- 4- 3- 2- 1 to push yourself forward and be bigger than your excuses.

Seeing the 5- 4- 3- 2- 1 countdown can serve as a vivid reminder of the Rule and its importance. Art hung the numbers on his office wall to keep him motivated and moving forward all day at work:

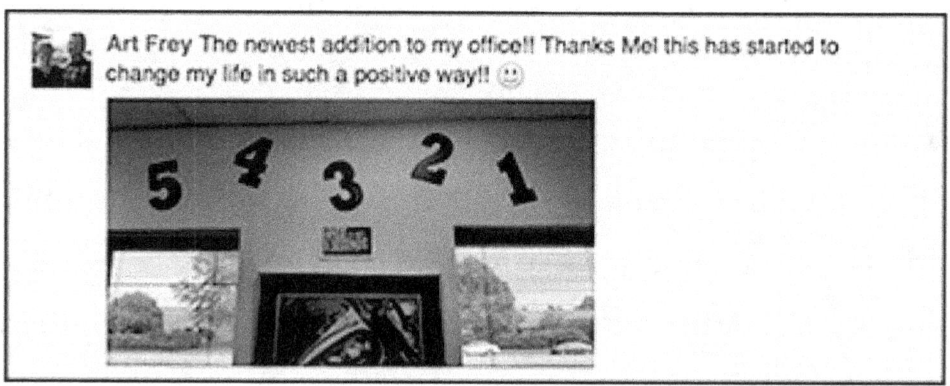

Can the Rule Create Lasting Behavior Change Too?

The Rule will beat the brain's operating system to help you win the battle with resistance in the moment. But do you know what else? Over time, as you repeat the Rule, you destroy that system all together. One thing most of us don't realize is that patterns of thinking like worrying, self-doubt, and fear are all just habits—and you repeat these thought patterns without even realizing it. If everything you do to sabotage your happiness is a habit, that means you can follow the latest research to break the habits of:

Waiting

Doubting

Holding back

Staying silent

Feeling insecure

Avoiding

Worry

Overthinking

There is a "Golden Rule of Habits" and it is very simple: In order to change any bad habit, you must replace the behavior pattern that you repeat. I will explain this in detail in Part 4 of the book. I'll teach you how to end the mental habits of worrying, anxiety, panic, and fear using the #5SecondRule in combination with all the latest research.

For now, what you need to know is this—the #5SecondRule and its countdown trick, 5- 4- 3- 2- 1- GO, will become your new behavior pattern. Instead of holding back, you'll 5- 4- 3- 2- 1 to push forward. The countdown is also what researchers call a "starting ritual." Starting rituals interrupt your bad default patterns and trigger new, positive patterns.

If you master the Rule you will reprogram your mind. You will teach yourself new behavior patterns. Instead of defaulting to worry, hesitation, and fear, you will find yourself automatically acting with courage. Over time, as you take more and more steps forward, you'll discover something else—real confidence and pride in yourself. The authentic kind that comes when you honor your goals and accomplish small wins that are important to you.

Everything that you think might be set in stone, including your habits, mindset, and personality are flexible. The implications of this for your life are absolutely thrilling. You can change your "default" mental settings and your habits one five-second decision at a time. Those small decisions add up to major changes in who you are, what you feel, and how you live.

Change your decisions and you'll change your life. And what will change your decisions more than anything? Courage.

**If you have the courage to start,
you have the courage to succeed.**

PART2

THE POWER OF COURAGE

CHAPTER FIVE

EVERYDAY COURAGE

"I HAVE LEARNED OVER THE YEARS

THAT WHEN ONE'S MIND IS MADE, THIS DIMINISHES

FEAR; KNOWING WHAT MUST BE DONE DOES AWAY WITH FEAR."

ROSA PARKS

Before I discovered the #5SecondRule, if you had asked me to give you examples of courage, I would have given you a list of history makers. I would never have said that courage is what it takes some days to get out of bed, speak to your boss, pick up the phone, or step on a scale. I would have told you that courage is a word used to describe acts of huge bravery.

Courageous people, in my view, were the Nobel Prize winners Malala Yousafzai, Leymah Gbowee, the Dalai Lama, Aung San Suu Kyi, Nelson Mandela, and Elie Wiesel. I would have thought about Winston Churchill and Britain standing up to fight against Nazi Germany, Rosa Parks standing up for her right to keep her seat on the bus, and Muhammad Ali steadfast in his religious beliefs and refusing to fight in Vietnam. I would have been reminded of Helen Keller, who triumphed over her own disabilities to advance the rights of others; of Sir Ernest Shackleton, who overcame shocking odds to rescue the crew of the *Endurance*; or of Galileo, who challenged the Orthodox Church to advance science.

But after using the Rule for seven years and hearing from so many people around the world, I have learned a very important certainty: Everyday life is full of moments that are scary, uncertain, and difficult. Facing these moments and unlocking the opportunity, magic, and joy in your life requires tremendous courage.

Courage is precisely what the #5SecondRule gives you. The Rule gave Jose the courage to believe in his value and ask for a raise.

Once he asked for one and got it, and there was a surprise waiting in his next paycheck—a bigger one.

Unexpected Love! What a great shout out. Thank you very much. I love you too. My currency holders surprised me a week later. When I looked at my check they added a dollar. Making a total of a 3 dollar raise! I was surprised. I thought of what he said during our conversation, "You're too valuable", with no hesitation he agreed on the $2 I asked for. Reading and philosophy has given me courage and balance. Again thank you very much. Best of luck! I am here if you ever need me. Your friend, Jose

The Rule gave Bryce the courage to put two years into writing and publishing a cookbook. And he didn't stop there. He got Barnes and Noble to host a book signing. As Bryce puts it, "you can achieve anything that you are passionate about and are willing to work for."

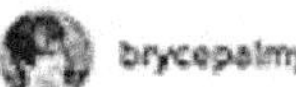

What's even cooler? Bryce was only 15 at the time!

The Rule helped Martin push through nine years of "one excuse after another" and slamming "on those brakes hard" to go back to school and pursue a second master's degree that will give him a more fulfilling career.

Subject: TedX: How to Stop Screwing Yourself Over

Message: Hi Mel,

I have watched your TedX presentation earlier this evening and found it to be funny, enlightening and most of all it gave me a lot of food for thought.

Having suffered with depression and anxiety issues since graduating University in my 30's I have slammed on those breaks hard for the last 9 years coming up with one excuse after another not to go on and peruse a Masters degree and have since been stuck in basic administration roles.

I have taken your advice, dug my old course books out so I can brush up on my previous studies and have started looking online for a suitable Masters degree.

Thank you for giving me the kick up the arse I needed. I know I'm just at the bottom of the mountain and I am just taking my first steps and know I'll stumble, but I now know that there inspirational people like yourself I can refer back to to get my moving again.

Many thanks.

Juanita learned to listen to her inner wisdom. Instead of "thinking" about a job search and a company her friend recommended, she picked up the phone and called "right now"—and guess what she got? Exactly what she pushed herself to go and get—a dream job.

Juanita
View Profile

5 second rule story- I've been doing a lot of soul searching, looking for a new job, asking myself what did i want - i stopped telling myself i was fine with my current position. I could no longer deny the fact that i wanted, needed and deserved more. My friend mentioned a company to me for the 3rd time. I had listened to you TED talk and told her I was going to hang up the phone and call that company right now. AND I DID! End result i now have a new job with that company. It is better than any other job I have interviewed for!

I started last week! 5 second rule - ROCKS! Thank you! Juanita

Learning about the #5SecondRule was a turning point for Gabe. After realizing "that I was responsible for everything that happened in my life," Gabe used the Rule to change his life by starting his own Virtual Reality company. Today, he is creating the career of his dreams.

Gabe

Went from a full time marketing manager who was "doing fine," to a connected, dedicated and growing owner of my own Virtual Reality company on my way to fulfilling the career of my dreams.

I was OK with being FINE, I forgot that I was responsible for everything that happened in my life.

Kristin's life has been forever changed because her boyfriend now has a way to battle his drug addiction. Whenever he feels the desire to go "back to one of those drugs," he uses the #5SecondRule to fight his addiction and retrain his mind. He counts backwards 5- 4- 3- 2- 1 to himself to trigger new behavior and "his mindset completely changes and he goes about his day."

Hello,

I saw you at the Scentsy Family Reunion this past summer. My boyfriend and I were in the audience. This story is more about him then me. You have forever changed our lives with the 5-4-3-2-1 rule. He is a recovering drug addict that most people don't know about. Well he finally stopped all the different drugs right before we left for our trip to Nashville, where we saw you. Since that day he uses your 5-4-3-2-1 rule every time he has a desire to go back to one of those drugs. He says it to himself and his mindset completely changes and he goes about his day. Thank you from the bottom of my heart, thank you for sharing your story.

Courage is, in fact, what I needed to get out of bed. It was scary to get out of bed because it meant facing my problems. It was difficult to look myself in the mirror and accept the fact that I was 41 years old and my life and career were in pretty lousy shape. It was overwhelming to consider I might not be able to fix the situation my husband and I were in.

Courage is what my daughter needs to put down the pen in her high school history class and raise her hand. It's what your team needs to escalate its concerns to you and it's what your kids need to tell you what's *really* going on. Putting your online profile up on a dating site or blocking your ex on your phone can feel like an act of bravery. So can adopting new technology for your business or walking in the door of your home and facing your problems head-on instead of pouring a drink and zoning out in front of the TV.

As I began to write this book and started collecting stories of people around the world using the Rule, it became clear that inside every decision there exist five seconds of courage that can change everything in our lives.

The more the word "courage" came up, the more I began to wonder if there was something about one of the most historic moments of courage that would help me better understand the nature of courage itself. The first person that came to mind was Rosa Parks. You probably know the story of how Rosa Parks sparked the modern American Civil Rights Movement on a chilly December evening in 1955 when she quietly refused to give up her seat on the bus for a white passenger.

Her moment of courage teaches us all that it's not the big moves that change everything—it's the smallest ones in your everyday life that do. She didn't plan to do what she did that night. Mrs. Parks described herself as the kind of person who tried to "be as careful as possible to stay out of trouble." The only thing she planned on doing that evening was to get home after a long day at work and have dinner with her husband. It was just an evening, like any other evening—until one decision changed everything.

Curious, I dug in and researched everything I could find about Mrs. Parks, from the National Archives, biographies, radio interviews, and newspaper articles. What I found is incredible. Just weeks after her arrest, she gave a radio interview to Sidney Rogers on Pacifica Radio and the National Archives website has a recording of it. Here's how she described that historic moment in her own words:

> *As the bus proceeded out of town on the third stop, the white passengers had filled the front of the bus. When I got on the bus, the rear was filled with colored passengers, and they were beginning to stand. The seat I occupied was the first of the*

seats where the Negro passengers, uh, take as they—on this route. The driver noted that the front of the bus was filled with white passengers, and there would be two or three men standing.

He looked back and…demanded the seats that we were occupying. The other passengers very reluctantly gave up their seats. But I refused to do so…The driver said that if I refused to leave the seat, he would have to call the police. And I told him, "Just call the police."

Then the radio interviewer asked her the million-dollar question:

"What in the world ever made you decide to be the person who after all these years of Jim Crowe and segregation, what made you at that particular moment decide you were going to keep that seat?"

She replied very simply,

"I felt that I was not being treated right and that I had a right to retain the seat that I had taken as a passenger on that bus."

He pressed her again noting that she had been mistreated for years, and wanted to know *what made her decide in that moment*—and in the interview, she paused for a second and then said:

"The time had just come that I had been pushed as far as I stand to be pushed, I suppose."

He asked her if she planned it—and she said,

"No."

He asked her if it just sort of happened. She agreed that it "just sort of happened."

This is a critical detail: *Rosa Parks didn't hesitate or think it through.* It happened so fast, she just listened to her instincts telling her *"I was not being treated right,"* and she pushed herself to follow them.

Since she didn't hesitate, there was no time to talk herself out of it.

Coincidentally, four days later, in that same city of Montgomery, Alabama, on December 5, 1955, there was another five-second decision that changed history.

The Montgomery Improvement Association was formed in response to Mrs. Parks' arrest and a 26-year-old black preacher was voted by his peers to lead the 381-day bus boycott that ensued. On being nominated to lead the boycott that night, the young preacher would later write:

"It happened so quickly that I did not have time to think it through. It is probable that if I had, I would have declined the nomination."

Thank goodness he didn't think it through. He would become one of the greatest civil rights leaders of all time. His name was Dr. Martin Luther King Jr.

Dr. King was pushed into the spotlight by his peers. Rosa pushed herself. They both experienced the power of a push. It's a moment when your instincts, values, and goals align, and you move so quickly you don't have time or a valid reason to stop yourself.

Your heart speaks and you don't think, you listen to what your heart tells you to do. Greatness is not a personality trait. It's inside all of us and sometimes it's hard for us to see it. Mrs. Parks was described by all who knew her as quiet and shy, and Dr. King famously struggled with self-doubt and fear in the beginning days of the Civil Rights movement.

Reflecting back on the radio that night in 1956, Mrs. Parks said, *"I hadn't thought I would be the person to do this, it hadn't occurred to me."* It probably hasn't occurred to you either what great things you might be capable of achieving at work and in your lifetime. Her example shows us that we are all more than capable of finding the courage to "act out of character" when the moment matters.

It is true, as Rosa Parks explained on air in that 1956 interview, that she was pushed *"as far as I could stand to be pushed"* by a system of discrimination. But in that singular moment, she was pushed forward by something way more powerful: herself.

That's what courage is. It's a push. The kind of push we give ourselves when we stand up, speak up, show up, go first, raise our hand or do whatever feels hard, scary, or uncertain. Do not look at our heroes in history, business, art, and music and assume that somehow they are different than you. It's not true.

Courage is a birthright. It is inside each and every one of us. You were born with it and you can tap into it anytime you want. It's not a matter of confidence, education, status, personality, or profession. It's simply a matter of knowing how to find it when you need it. And when you need it, you'll probably be alone.

It's going to be just you sitting in a meeting at work, standing in your kitchen, riding the subway, looking at your phone, staring at your computer, or thinking about something—and all of sudden, it will happen. Something will go down, and your instincts will come alive. You'll have an urge to act. Your values and your instincts will tell you what you *should* do. And your feelings will scream "NO." That is the push moment. You don't have to have all the answers. You just have to make a decision in the next five seconds.

Dan is alone at his computer thinking about registering for summer classes. He wants to earn his college degree but at the age of 44, the idea of starting as a freshman is nothing short of terrifying.

Courage is what Christine needs as she's sitting in a marketing meeting in Plano, Texas. She has a great idea to share but wonders, *Is this going to sound stupid?*

Tom is standing in a bar in Chicago. The moment he sees her he can't look away. He can either turn back toward his friends and pretend to care about the football game they're discussing, or find the courage to start walking toward her.

The entire sales organization of a financial software company feels discouraged in Nashville. They've hit their numbers three years in a row, and quotas just got raised yet again.

Alice in England needs to push herself out the door to go on a run. She's inspired by her friend on Facebook, but *feels discouraged* by how long it's been since she last exercised.

Halfway around the world, Patel can't stop thinking about a friend whose son just died in a car accident. He doesn't know what to say, and the thought of losing his own son terrifies him. He tells himself, *It will be easier if I wait a few days,* but the urge to pick up the phone, stop by the house…*to do something* lingers.

In China, Sy has just signed on as a distributor for a new skin care line. She has at least a dozen people she wants to call. She looks at her phone and hesitates—*what if they think I'm being pushy?*

In Queensland, Australia, Todd knows exactly what he wants to do with his life, and it isn't studying law, it's physical education. But before Todd can take control of his future, he'll need to face his parents' disappointment.

And Mark is lying in bed in Auckland, Australia, where it's 10:30 p.m. He turns and looks at his wife as she reads her book. He would love to make love to her, but he assumes she's not in the mood; he wants to lean over and kiss her shoulder but he *fears rejection.* He needs courage to lean toward her after so many months of feeling like her roommate.

These stories are real and they are just the tip of the iceberg. They highlight the struggle between our desire to change our lives and our fear of it. They also reveal the power that everyday courage has to transform everything.

Seth Godin once wrote "a different part of our brains is activated when we think about what's possible rather than what's required." I believe the same is true when we think about being courageous, rather than focusing on the fears that stop us. It's the difference between focusing on the solution rather than the problem, and that tiny switch is mentally liberating.

There's something powerful about framing my struggle to get out of bed, Patel's struggle to call his friend, a sales organization's struggle to embrace a higher sales goal, and Alice's struggle to exercise as acts of everyday courage.

After all, courage is just a push.

When you push yourself, you may not change the world, the laws, or spark a civil rights movement but I can guarantee you'll change something equally as important—you'll change yourself.

There is only one YOU.

And there will never be another one.

That's your power.

CHAPTER SIX

WHAT ARE YOU WAITING FOR?

"THE TIME IS ALWAYS RIGHT TO DO WHAT IS RIGHT."

DR. MARTIN LUTHER KING, JR

Tom is celebrating a new piece of business with his colleagues at Stetson's Steakhouse inside the Hyatt Regency Hotel in downtown Chicago. He is crushing his quota for the year and the win today will put the territory he manages ahead on the leaderboard. Four months ago, he threw himself into his job at a financial tech company after his wife moved out. It's been a welcome distraction as he tries to pick up the pieces of his personal life. He turns toward the bartender to order another round, and that's when he sees her.

She's standing just across the bar, laughing with her friends. There's something about her. He can't quite put his finger on it. He thinks about walking over and talking to her, but he hesitates. He starts to wonder if it's too soon to put himself out there. He begins to feel uncertain: *Would a woman that hot go for a guy with two kids?*

Tom has a decision to make and he'll make it in the next five seconds.

In the amount of time it takes to start walking across a bar, Tom could start to rebuild his life. In the amount of time it takes to raise your hand in a meeting, you can change how you are perceived at work. In the amount of time it takes to open your mouth and compliment someone, you could brighten someone's day. And if you don't, the moment will pass, like it did for Blake and now she wants to "kick myself."

Whatever reason you use to hold yourself back—you are wrong. It's not safer to stay quiet. It's not better to keep the peace. It's not futile to try. It's not risky. You are wrong. All your excuses and reasons are wrong. There is no "right time" to improve your life. The moment you move you'll discover your strength. That's the way to bring the REAL you to the table—by pushing the *real* you out of your head and into the world. And the best time to do it, is right now when your heart tells you to move.

We waste so much of our lives waiting for the right time to have the conversation, ask for the raise, bring it up, or start things. It reminds me of that famous Wayne Gretzky quote: *"You miss 100% of the shots you don't take."* Here's the thing—you never regret the shots you do take but you always regret holding back. Anthony realized this the hard way:

Life is already hard, yet we make it so much harder when we listen to our fears, we convince ourselves to wait, and we hold our greatest selves back. We all do it. And not just in bars. We hold ourselves back at work, at home, and in our relationships.

The question is, why do we do this? The answer is brutal. You can call it a fear of rejection, or a fear of failure, or a fear of looking bad. The reality is, we hide because we are afraid even to try.

I had a conversation a few months ago with my daughter Kendall that illustrates just how deadly this waiting game can be to your dreams. To give you some background, Kendall is fifteen and a very talented singer. From the moment she wakes up until the moment she goes to bed, she's singing.

Recently, one of her mentors recommended her for an audition with the directors of a musical in New York City. He had placed kids on tour with *Les Misérables, Mary Poppins,* and *Matilda.* He thought Kendall had a very good chance of landing a role.

The second the topic came up, she said she "wanted to audition" but never wrote her mentor back about it. I asked her why she was waiting. It was fascinating and heartbreaking to hear how her thoughts and feelings had trapped her. Funny enough, she wasn't afraid of the audition itself. At least not when she thought about it. It was everything that *might happen* after the audition.

She said that she didn't want to try out because, "What if I didn't make it, Mom? What if I am not as good as I think I am? If I don't audition, at least I can tell myself that I'm amazing—I'm just too lazy to have what I want."

Now we were getting somewhere. The fear of sucking, of not being good enough, of feeling like a loser—none of us wants to face that reality. So we avoid it like the plague. I actually do it with exercise. I can pretend I'm in decent shape as long as I avoid it. The moment I hit the gym I have to face reality. And the reality is that within two minutes of running on a treadmill, I have to go the bathroom and I'm out of breath. I'm not in great shape at all. I have a lot of work to do. That's why we dodge challenges—to protect our egos, even if it means eliminating the possibility of getting what we want.

I listened to Kendall talk about her fear that she wasn't good enough, and then asked her one simple question:

"What If You're Wrong?"

It's a powerful question, and we don't ask it nearly enough. What if you're wrong? What if you audition and you really are as good as everyone says? What if your idea actually is the next million-dollar business? What if you not only meet your quota again this year, but you also actually surpass it? What if being single isn't as scary as you think and your true soulmate is just days away from bumping into you? Are you really going to let your worries stop you from doing the work, having the love life, and being your greatest self? You damn well better not.

And even if you do suck—there's another thing you can say to yourself:

So What!?

So what if you suck? At least you tried. As far as I'm concerned landing the role is irrelevant. Just like the woman Tom saw at the bar is irrelevant. The only thing relevant is *you*. The power is *inside* of you. The only way you access that power is pushing yourself to try. The greatest you shows up at the audition, walks up to the gal or guy at the bar, and raises their hand and their voice at work.

You'll never stop yourself from starting to worry about something. But you can stop yourself from letting those worries drag you into a parade of worries that take control of your mind. You can assert yourself and push yourself to think about something empowering. You step back into the present moment and go for what you want. And you can do it in five seconds flat.

We are all guilty of thinking about getting involved but not doing it. We're all waiting "for the right time." It's total stupidity. In a recent survey, 85% of professional services employees admitted they were withholding critical feedback from their bosses. Why? You already know the answer—they're waiting for the "right time." The same is true for your kids, your spouse, your friends, and your colleagues.

All human beings are wired this way. One of the most insightful and enlightening aspects of Adam Grant's incredible book *Originals: How Non-Conformists Move the World* is when he describes how some our greatest heroes are just like us in this simple regard: they hesitated, doubted themselves, and almost missed the opportunities of their lifetimes because they didn't feel ready. I find it reassuring to know that the people we admire most needed to be pushed through their fears, excuses, and feelings, just like you and me.

You know Michelangelo, the artist who painted the Sistine Chapel in Rome? There's a backstory you might not know. According to Grant, when the Pope asked Michelangelo to paint the Sistine Chapel in 1506, Michelangelo felt so overwhelmed with self-doubt that he not only wanted to wait, but he also actually fled to Florence and hid. The Pope had to stalk Michelangelo and pester him for two years to get him to agree to paint it.

Want to hear another one? How about one related to Apple? In 1977, when an investor offered Steve Jobs and Steve Wozniak funding to launch Apple, Wozniak felt so afraid and uncertain he wanted to "wait a while" before he quit his job. He didn't *feel* ready. He was pushed by "Jobs, multiple friends, and his own parents" to make the leap.

Remember the stories in the last chapter about Dr. Martin Luther King Jr admitting he would have declined the nomination to lead the Montgomery Improvement Association "had he thought it through"? Or Rosa Parks' admission that she never thought "she would be the one to do this"? In the moment, neither one of them stopped to think. They didn't wait to *feel* ready. That's what we all need to do. We are all capable of greatness. I believe that. It is our feelings and fears that convince us now is not the right time and keep us from achieving greatness.

Grant then writes this line in his book, which made my heart feel heavy: "We can only imagine how many Wozniaks, Michelangelos, and Kings never pursued, publicized, or promoted their original ideas because they were not dragged or catapulted into the spotlight." The question to ask yourself is this one:

What Are You Waiting For?

Are you waiting for someone to ask you, drag you, pick you, or catapult you into the spotlight, or are you willing to find the courage to push yourself? Are you waiting to feel ready? Waiting for the right time. Waiting to gain confidence. Waiting to feel like it. Waiting to feel worthy. Waiting until you have more experience.

Sometimes there is no next time, no second chance, or no time out. Stop waiting. It's now or never. When you wait, you aren't procrastinating. You are doing something more dangerous. You are deliberately convincing yourself "now is not the time." You are actively working against your dreams.

Paula could have convinced herself that she would "never qualify" for a great job opportunity. She would have been very wrong.

I just applied for a job I never thought I would qualify for because I figured, "why not just try it?" I didn't focus on my shortcomings but emphasized my qualities and got the job. Previously I would have forgotten about it after 5 seconds and not even tried by the way ;–)

—Paula

By "emphasizing her qualities" instead of focusing on her shortcomings, Paula was able to push past her fears and land the job.

You may think you're protecting yourself from judgment, rejection, or upsetting someone, but when you make excuses and talk yourself into waiting, you are limiting your ability to make your dreams come true. I'm amazed by how much time I've wasted in my life waiting for the right time, waiting until I'm sure, waiting until I think my work is perfect, or waiting until I feel like it.

You may be afraid of finding out that you suck, like my daughter was. Let me tell you what really sucks: being older and regretting that you never went for it. Being 30 and realizing you let fear of what your friends thought keep you from ever really putting yourself out there when you were younger. Friends, by the way, who you never talk to anymore. Being 56 and realizing you should have divorced your spouse ten years ago. Being 45 and wishing you had had the courage to take on a project at work that you now realize would have changed the trajectory of your career. Or sitting in college classes earning a degree to please your parents when knowing in your heart that you want to be doing something else with your life.

There is no right time. There is only right now. You get one life. This is it. And it's not going to begin again. It's up to you to push yourself to make the most of it and the time to do it is right now.

You Validate Your Ideas By Pursuing Them

It's heartbreaking to hear from so many of you with a creative idea or product concept that are waiting for someone else to validate it. It's so sad because waiting for validation will be the death of your dreams. If you have an idea for a show or a book, and you are waiting for an executive at a TV network or a publishing house to pick you, you will lose. It's like Tom in the bar hoping his soulmate will just walk up to him and pick him. Or me waiting until I felt motivated to wake up and get out of bed. Waiting until you are ready will not make it happen. The world doesn't work that way.

The world rewards those who are courageous enough to stop waiting and start. If you dream of being on television, I can tell you from first-hand experience that the TV executive you hope discovers you is actually on YouTube right now looking for someone who didn't wait. The person who has the courage to start, create, and put themselves and their ideas out there is the one who will win.

The only difference between that idea for a novel you want to write and British author E.L. James who wrote the blockbuster *Fifty Shades of Gray* trilogy (that was devoured by nearly every woman on the planet Earth and sold a million copies in four days) is the fact that she didn't wait for permission, the right time, or to feel ready. She didn't wait until she had a book deal. In fact, she started writing erotica on a Twilight-themed blog! She found the courage to start in small ways, and put herself out there over and over until she built the confidence to write a book. And

Fifty Shades of Gray was that book. It was self-published by a working mom who wrote in her free time. Yup.

By the way, that's also how Grammy award-winning musician Ed Sheeran got discovered. He was 15 years old playing songs in a park in England with no permit and no guarantee that anyone would notice. That's how you do it. You push yourself to get out of your comfort zone and you begin. There is no other way. You stop waiting for "the right time" and you start. That's how award-winning *Broad City* landed its hit show on Comedy Central. They acted with courage and started filming 3-minute clips on an iPhone and posting them on YouTube.

And every single YouTube star, from Tyler Oakley, to make-up tutorial phenom Michelle Phan, to "My Drunk Kitchen" host Hannah Hart, to Minecraft narrator "Stampy Cat," will tell you that if they had told themselves to wait until they felt ready or until they had a sponsor, they would still be living a boring life instead creating a life of their dreams and laughing all the way to the bank.

Waiting, thinking, and "almost doing it" don't count. As Kyra explains, to change anything you actually have to do it. #AlmostDoesntCount

Kyra

5,4,3,2,1 Go! I almost didn't go to the "block party" my complex held last night because I was exhausted after work... I almost decided not to donate blood at the truck they had there... I almost didn't make the exposure to the nice nurse I met who was also donating, I almost didn't run back to my apartment to get my third party tools to give to her before I left. I almost didn't follow up with her this morning and when she invited me over to go talk to her and her girlfriends about it? I almost didn't go because I was still in my PJ's, had no expert lined up and felt unprepared... But I did and now? I will be entering 2 new PC's tonight and 2 tomorrow and I'm officially NLC qualified for September and am now half way through October! The moral of the story is #almostdoesntcount #justdoit

The difference between people who make their dreams come true and those of us who don't is just one thing: the courage to start and the discipline to keep going.

The Rule is a game-changer because it 5- 4- 3- 2- 1 forces you to get out of your head and start and it'll 5- 4- 3- 2- 1 help you keep going.

And that brings us back to Tom at the bar in the Hyatt Regency in Chicago. Will he start walking toward the girl across the room or decide to wait? Well…that depends. It depends on who is making the decision for Tom. Will it be Tom's heart that makes the decision or his head? Will it be Tom's dreams that win or will it be his fears? Rosa Parks offers some amazing advice for moments like this one—Tom needs to do what *"must be done."* Tom knows in his heart what must be done. He needs to start living again.

Waiting won't help. Waiting will only make it worse. When you sit with fear and uncertainty your mind makes it expand; it's called "the spotlight effect" and it's one of the many tricks your brain plays in an attempt to keep you "safe."

The fear Tom feels is real. The uncertainty is scary. The self-doubt can be crippling. No one wants to be rejected or feel like a fool. No one wants to find out that they "suck."

That's why the moment right before you walk into a networking meeting, a party, an interview, a cafeteria, or start walking toward someone you find attractive, it can feel daunting. We think about what could go wrong or how awkward it will feel if no one welcomes us, instead of all the possibilities.

But safety isn't what Tom wants. Tom wants to rebuild his life and find love again and that's going to take courage. As scary as it is taking that first step to the other side of the bar, Tom is about to discover that all the magic, wonder, and joy in life happens the moment he does.

You can feel uncertain and be ready. You can be afraid and do it anyway. You can fear rejection and still go for it.

Five Seconds of Courage Changes Everything

Tom starts counting to himself, "5- 4- 3-…" and by the time he gets to 2, he starts walking across the room. He has no idea what he'll say to her. His heart is racing, but for the first time in a long time he doesn't feel numb, he feels alive. The closer he gets to her, the more his heart races. She turns around just as he reaches her. What happens next is…irrelevant.

It doesn't matter what happens because she either becomes his soulmate or she doesn't. The ending of the story is irrelevant—the *only* thing that matters is the beginning of the story, that Tom made a choice to begin living again. That's how you listen to your heart. Whether you are starting to date again, starting a company, or starting a YouTube channel, you must find the courage to start.

Notice how we desperately want an assurance that Tom "got the girl." It makes for a great movie plot, but "getting the girl" isn't the point. Life isn't a Nicholas Sparks novel. Life is gritty and hard and then suddenly it is brilliant and amazing. Besides, the girl could be engaged. She could be gay. She could be a real bitch. Even if she's amazing and they end up having crazy hot sex or go on to get married, "the girl" is not the source of power in the story. Tom is.

The treasure in your life is buried within *you*. It's not inside of someone else. Tom is the source of power in his life and you are the source of power in yours. You unlock that power when you listen to your instincts and 5- 4- 3- 2- 1 push yourself to honor them. When you discover your "inner true self" it will be the "most important gift of all."

Melody Fowler I have used the 5 sec rule everyday (multiple times) since Dallas! It has helped me clear out negative thoughts, it has helped me reach out to people and start conversations I might not initiate otherwise, it has brought my inner true self out loud! And that to me has been the most important gift of all, to be me and show my daughter how to do it too! Thank you Mel!

Jean-Baptiste also saw this. He wrote to me that he realized "that nobody was going to come and get me to live the life that I want to live and that taking action is the only way to create my own space into the world."

Jean-Baptiste

Hello! I just wanted to let you know that i admire the work you do and the ideas you share with world. I'm 19 years old, and watching your ted talk and your other speeches allowed me to realize that nobody was going to come and get me to live the life that i want to live and that taking action is the only way to create my own space into the world. I believe that everybody could bring something new and original to the world we live in. Seriously, you helped. Thank you for that. Keep changing the world one sequin at time.

With love, JB.

Just as Jean-Baptiste said, I also "believe that everybody could bring something new and original to the world we live in." The potential for massive greatness exists inside every single one of us.

The way that you activate the power of you is by finding the courage you need every single day to push yourself forward. When you listen to your instincts (*"get up and face the day, Mel," "suck it up and start walking, Tom," "take care of your nephews, Catherine," "don't give up your seat, Rosa"*)—it's clear what you must do.

There is no debate when you follow what's inside your heart. The only thing that will quiet the chatter in your head is a decision to move. As I said in the very beginning of the book, you really are just one decision away from a completely different life.

We are all so afraid of uncertainty that we want a guarantee before we even try. We want evidence that if we take a risk we will "get the girl" too. Even if Tom gets the girl, it's not proof that you will. "Getting the girl" or "the guy," for that matter, is a numbers game. To play any game, you have to start. To win, you'll need to keep going. If you want to make your dreams come true, get ready for the long game.

Life is not a one-and-done sort of deal. You've got to work for what you want. Do you know the game Angry Birds? Rovio, the brand that created the game, launched 51 unsuccessful games before they developed Angry Birds. How about *The Avengers* star Mark Ruffalo? Do you know how many auditions he did before he landed his *first* role? Almost 600! Even Babe Ruth struck out 1,330 times. My favorite vacuum cleaner is a Dyson. And there's no wonder why it doesn't suck at sucking up the dirt. James Dyson created 5,127 prototypes! What? And this last one will blow your mind. Picasso created nearly 100 masterpieces in his lifetime. But what most people don't know is that he created a total of more than 50,000 works of art.

Did you see the last number? 50,000. That's two pieces of art a day. Success is a numbers game. And you're not going to win it if you keep telling yourself to wait. The more often that you choose courage, the more likely you'll succeed.

When you 5- 4- 3- 2- 1 push yourself forward you'll discover the magic in your life and you open yourself up to the world, to opportunity, and to possibility. You might not get the girl, the part, or the response you wanted but that's not the point. In the end, you'll get something way cooler—you'll discover the power inside of you.

Hold on. Let me over think about it.